Opening

The Poetry Society of the Open University

Annual Anthology

of

OU Poets

2024

Copyright remains with the individual poets.
All rights reserved.

Published 2024 by Open University Poets.

ISBN 978-1-7399361-3-6

Editor: Sue Spiers
Cover: Tay Boat at Newburgh by Ian Ledward
https://www.onemidshore.com/

Printed by Lulu.com

Introduction

OU Poets is the Poetry Society of the Open University. It is open to any student or staff member, past or present. At the time of going to press there are about 90 members from all over the U.K. with some in mainland Europe and worldwide.

Members of the society submit poems to a magazine, which is produced 5 times a year, each one having a different voluntary editor. The magazine is not a publication *per se* and is strictly produced by the members for the members. There is a section for comment and criticism of members' work.

At the end of the year, members are asked to vote for the 20 poems they most appreciated from the 5 magazines produced that year. Those with the most votes, allowing for no more than one poem per poet, appear in the following year's issue of Openings. The anthology is as broad-based as the society itself and reflects the varied backgrounds, interests and tastes of the members.

If you would like more information about OU Poets, please contact the Secretary:
      Karen Macfarlane
      secretary@oupoets.org.uk

or the Chair:
      Polly Stretton
      chair@oupoets.org.uk
      Tel: (+44) 1886 830054 for postal address information.

Or visit our website at http://www.oupoets.org.uk

      @OUPoets

Contents

Poem	Name	Page
Valentine 2023	John Starbuck	7
IN LOVE	Christine Frederick	8
I wrote only of flowers	Karen Macfarlane	10
On hearing Paul Simon's Diamonds On the Soles of her Shoes	Madeline Parsons	11
Jazz at the Royal - Now and Then	Adrian Green	12
Ars Poetica 2023	Peter Meredith-Smith	14
Poet at the Pageant	Pru Bankes Price	16
Irritable Poet Syndrome	Liz Beber	18
What do we do about a problem like me, eh?	Tim Field	19
One of them	Denis Ahern	20
ILLUSION	Suzie Millar	21
The Splendour of Socks	Susan Jarvis Bryant	22
in her shoes	Jane Avery	24
Salvage	Sue Spiers	25
THE DINNER JACKET	Kewal Paigankar	26
MY NIGHTMARE	John Hughes	28
Piss Dream	Ross McGivern	29
Reverie	Vicki Morley	31
Cœur Noir	Polly Stretton	33
Brown and blue hues of estuaries	Cate Cody	40
Sutton Hoo	Barbara Cumbers	41
She drinks	Jenny Hamlett	42

Contents

Poem	Name	Page
Climbers at Yosemite	Geoff Chilton	44
Changing seasons	Sally James	45
Cold Water	Nigel Kent	46
The Wriggling River	Ian Ledward	48
Reflection 2	Julie Anne Gilligan	50
all rules are suspended	M. C. Gardner	51
summer seasonal affective disorder	Marilyn Francis	52
TEATIME	Katherine Rawlings	54
Silver	Alice Harrison	55
The End	Ian Campbell	56
Wounded In Action	K. J. Barrett	58
Jubilation 1945	Wendy Goulstone	59
Gooseberry Pie	Jim Lindop	60
Grace	Phil Craddock	61
Negative Space	Kate Young	64
When Mother Died	Nigel Pearce	66
EXTINGUISHED?	Rob Lowe	67
IN DEATH	Hilary Mellon	68
Looking for Hardware	Julie Stamp	69
How the world can decrease and expand	Ali Chakir	70
Villanelle: Passing Through	Lindsay Rossdale	71
Poets Alphabetically by Surname		72
Acknowldgements		73

for Ian Ledward
(02/12/1946 – 10/11/2023)

John Starbuck

Valentine 2023

Love,
Do I love?
Until the ice has all left Nome;
Until the sea surrounds our home;
When trees are waving in the foam;
When salt has poisoned our good loam
And overwhelmed the fishing gnome;
The house is perching on a holm;
The cat is disinclined to roam;
My beard needs brushes, not a comb;
When all the popes have gone from Rome;
When Notlob is a palindrome;
'Til then,
You,
I'll love.

Christine Frederick

IN LOVE

I am in love.
In love with life.
I never thought.
To be a wife.
My being feels.
At ease and free.
My choices are simple.
All around me.
Listen to life.
Hear it sing.
See the swallows.
On the wing.
Hear the rustle.
Of petals fall.
From honeyed blossom.
On orchard wall.

I am in love.
In love with life.
I have no need.
To be a wife.
The world about me.
Billows and fills.
Clouds dance by.
Upon the hills.
Trees wave branches.
Full of flowers.
Water flows on.

For hours and hours.
The world drifts by.
Its energy so timeless.
I'm in love with life.
I must confess.

Karen Macfarlane

I wrote only of flowers
After K. J. Barrett

I wrote only of flowers
as magnolias never offend

filled pages with forget-me-nots
and sweet scentless lilies

turned my pen towards sunlight and gentle rain
while the ink inside was brewing a storm

believed roses were safe, then watched
as thorns grew from my fingers.

Madeline Parsons

On hearing Paul Simon's
Diamonds On The Soles of Her Shoes

Standing by the cooker, slicing carrots
for a casserole, a song I had not heard
in decades slithers from the radio and catches
me blind-sided. An image of our life together

blazes up inside me, fierce and trembling:
us, dancing round the kitchen, singing
along, word perfect: *people say I'm crazy
I got diamonds on the soles of my shoes.*

The music ends; the wobbling saucepan
rights itself again. But surely there were rows
back then, I think, promises not kept,
the sound of slamming doors? But, helpless

on the foothills of old age, the shadow
of the mountain blotting out the light,
it seems our life (improbable, I know) was full
of dancing, singing, hopeful, diamond bright.

Adrian Green

Jazz at The Royal – Now and Then

The open room with airy views
sits lightly on the memory
of smoke-filled cellar bars

where jazz sounds curled around
the darkened alcoves and the pillars
holding up the floor above,

the players timed their choruses
and breaks to cigarettes
left smouldering on music stands, while

sweat and smoke merged in an atmosphere
we did not know was there until
we came out to the early morning air,

but now we sit in comfort,
breathing clear, foot tapping
to those bebop tunes, and nodding

sagely to the sounds made classical
by passing time, their menace
calmed by intervening years.

This is the better world
we tell ourselves, while sipping
froth from our expensive beers.

The music is the same, though now
we hear it differently and cannot imagine
how our heirs will hear it in their time.

Peter Meredith-Smith

Ars Poetica 2023

Page or stage?
Read or said?
Open mic or bedside light?

Why should we care
how poetry is made or shown,
as long as something fires
when words are sown
by writers for readers
to reap and know,
through shining metaphors,
some different sense
of this world they share?

A seeing anew
to make them care afresh
about their lives and times:
novel insight
by the light
or burnished words.

Effulgent words,
revealing feelings fresh
about the loves and trials
of those dissonate makers,
the private partakers
in this cojoining art.

They who find and see,
who sense such mutuality,
in private, cloistered moments.

Precious moments,
made and shared apart,
engendered through this lyric art,

beyond the page,
beyond the stage,
far from the open mic,
long after the dousing
of the bedside light.

Pru Bankes Price

Poet at the Pageant

An anniversary was to be celebrated
the precise occasion sketchy but no matter
games and singing teachers were tasked
with creating an open-air production
telling the tale of our historic priory founded
by Augustinian monks but through a chequered
history now sanctified once more as a convent
run by nuns under guidance from the Good Shepherd.

Every pupil was to either sing, dance, recite
or simply tumble their way across the lawns
designated as a stage for the day,
the entire proceeding accompanied
by the large-bosomed piano teacher
thumping with gusto on an upright piano,
a little out of tune but nevertheless
wheeled outside for the day
with a plea to the Good Shepherd
for the blessing of a fine afternoon.

Best of all was the guest of honour;
a poet of grand reputation
(whispered as the next Poet Laureate)
was to honour every one of us with a visit.
By fortunate coincidence he lived close by.
That day expectations were high, the sun shone,
tension towered as our famous poet
made a smiling speech, settled into his deckchair
took out his handkerchief – fiddled and fidgeted
while Reverend Mother scowled askance until

finally, John Betjeman flourished that snowy handkerchief
now knotted at the corners
                settled it gently on his head
                                and fell
                                          asleep

Liz Beber

Irritable Poet Syndrome

It's all or nothing.

Brain bloated with ideas churning and wowling around.
Streams of matter come rushing and gushing unbidden,
semi-formed and punctuated with bits of rawness.
Irrepressible disturber of sleep, meetings and country walks

or it's clogged. It's in there, impacted, word-jammed
all bunged up and nowhere to go. Brain-straining gets nothing
moving save the odd little burst of hot air.

I suspect it's contagious.
Like-minded people describe the same symptoms.

There are definite triggers: those we have in common –
autumn, spring, love, death, having to wear glasses.
Then there's the idiosyncratic ones – the M62,
home perms and Volvo drivers.

There's no cure.

A healthy diet helps. A dose of Plum Duffy, a little nibble
                                              of John Éclair.
or a dollop of Ferlinghetti Bolognaise should keep you regular.

Failing that, a tincture of juniper and quinine
or a distillation of Scottish peat bog can help restore the flow.
Caution advised: too much, and these cerebral aperients
are liable to precipitate literary incontinence
and you're back to having to trot off,
find some paper, and let it all out…

Tim Field

What do we do about a problem like me, eh?

Roald Dahl rewritten and notecards with kittens.
Dogs in green fleeces, lost jigsaw pieces,
Trash TV tat that Saturday night brings,
These are a few of my least fav'rite things.

Long queues at Tesco, modern art frescoes,
Fake crafted gin and cars pushing in,
Knotweed and brambles, and insects that sting,
These are a few of my least fav'rite things.

Artisan jam, loud screaming pop fans,
False politicians, fanatic religion,
The very last bit when the large lady sings,
These are a few of my least fav'rite things.

Naff cookie adverts, phone pop-up inserts,
Squirrels on feeders are such cheeky bleeders,
Populist statements to which ev'ryone clings,
These are a few of my least fav'rite things.

Rude men that whistle; a boring epistle,
Christmas style jumpers and cars up your bumper,
Getting in the bath when the telephone rings,
These are a few of my least fav'rite things.

When my spleen vents,
Then my blood boils
And the shit hits the fan
Coz these are a few of my least fav'rite things
And I know that I'm just a grumpy old man.

Denis Ahern

One of them

(After 'Her Kind' by Anne Sexton)

I have been one of them,
those laddish buffoons,

misogynists who didn't know that word,
knee-jerked tongued, spitting a vile mix
of admiration and distain at blamelessness,
innocence deserving respect.

I have been one of them
and the memory hurts.

Suzie Millar

ILLUSION

I sit amongst you,
Physically close.

Lips move. Expressions change.
Bodies tense and relax.

Oddments of words reach me
but, how to make sense of it all?

An invisible barrier defeats me,
hides you from my world.

Like a mirage all is illusion.

In truth I am far away.

Susan Jarvis Bryant

The Splendour of Socks

I do not give a nibbled fig,
  A bucking-bullock's toss,
An elf owl's hoot, a pixie's jig,
  A dippy hippo's dross,
A Casanova's roving eye,
  A portly warthog's waddle,
A braying ass's rasping cry
  For blowhards blasting twaddle.

I do not give a rubber duck,
  A box of poxy frogs,
A plucky chicken's lick of luck,
  A podgy jogger's clogs,
A loafing gopher's oafish fit,
  A boozer's crimson snitch,
A feckless speck, a witless whit
  For twits that itch to bitch.

I do not give a donkey's conk,
  An armadillo's armour,
A dandy gander's randy honk,
  A barmy llama's karma,
A flirty turtle's fancy shell,
  A chipper puppy's yap,
A howler monkey's yell form hell
  For cretins spouting crap.

I yearn to hear a word of cheer,
   A joke that stokes a grin,
A ditty from a balladeer
   To ring beyond the din
Of cakeholes keen to caterwaul
   And shock around the clock.
I'm set to lob all gobs that bawl
   A bunkum-blocking sock.

Jane Avery

In her shoes

shoes lined with cardboard
toe to heel
embroidered elbows
patched skinny knees
I have been her kind

laced social shoes
unpatented
a uniform a co-op grant
a coat of many colours
I have been her kind

the shoes that walked another road
heel to toe
to find a space
where she might fit   exhale perhaps
I have been her kind

Sue Spiers

Salvage

School blouses on the washing line, hung a hundred times, belt-worn waists, sweat stained armpits and all too small for the youngest child, become waste.

The farmer's dungarees, earthy from planting where he rubs his hands in and out of pockets, palms on his knees before food, will be waste.

Small white flowers on her dancing dress, too loved to be discarded, its hem droops and seams loosen, something must be saved or it's a waste.

Mother has darned patches, rehemmed edges, reclaimed the bits she can from her basket of scraps until there's not enough to prevent waste.

A bargain, end-of-line, blue thread from the haberdashery shop, her eye on cream wool and a thick, steel needle, otherwise more waste.

Baby's cotton rompers, linen pyjamas and curtain hemp are quilted: a multitude of squares and oblongs, sewn sashiko style from waste.

Sun-faded shades are bathed in a tub of washy indigo dye to preserve the patterns of the fabrics, then it's sluiced out as waste.

Six foot by four foot; a bedspread of many layers – more years' use until it's framed, its craft revered as appreciation of waste.

Kewal Paigankar

THE DINNER JACKET

Thrown overboard for not wearing a dinner jacket
Playing duff notes on the piano
Holding cutlery the wrong way round
Not smoothing the creases on the napkins at the tables;
Singing out of tune on New Year's night
Missing his cue as the bingo announcer
Unwittingly treading on trailing silk gowns
While carrying the drinks tray;
Spinning the roulette wheel with too much force
Fluffing his numbers at the casino table
Being drunk while on lookout duty on deck
Giving wrong directions
When manning the Information Desk.

He swears revenge while going down deep
Miles and fathoms past the exotic fauna
Till he comes to rest on the ocean floor
Next to the wrecked hulls of old ships
With their starboards and sails still intact.
He rises like Kraken, a towering gargantuan monolith
Drinking the oceans dry to quench his thirst
Till he has changed the topography of the world.
No more oceans and seas; there is only land.
Pursing his lips, tired from the exertions
He rests on the dry surface,
His face forming a smile.

And the smile is wide,
Wide as the deep oceans
North to South, East to West,
Until it covers all land mass
And the whole of the universe.

He remembers to wear the dinner jacket.

John Hughes

MY NIGHTMARE

I am an ancient bugger,
My thochts are oot o'date
I dinna' read a book noo
And jist get up at eight.

I hardly look at papers
But gawk at Sky TV
I love my blinkin' fitba,
And no' much else you see.

I used to dae my gairden
But noo I have a flat
My wife and family members
Have made me see tae that.

I've set this tae a guid tune
I heard on BBC
I canna mind noo if it wiz
On radio or TV!

Ross McGivern

Piss Dream

Piss Dream: intense dream that wakes you between 2-3AM causing you to grope for meaning. However, there is no meaning, the reality is it's your bladder waking you up from a deep sleep.

Last night I dreamed of father,
he'd come to watch me spew some words.
He sat apart from the crowd
on a rigid plastic municipal chair.

His suit was green-tinged, white linen
and he wore a haystack of hair.
His face was blurred at the edges
but his nose was certainly his nose.

He wanted to talk.
I should have listened.
He wanted to hug
but the chatter of others pulled me away.

In dreams
I am as brittle a son
as I was in reality.

The knocking of doors,
Him calling my name.
The stammering tongue

The forgetting of lines.
The twinge of the bladder
awake/lost at sea.

Despite searching dark corridors
he was gone.

He never saw me speak.

I never said –

Vicki Morley

Reverie

The colours sing in your dreams,
lifting the corrugated iron roof,
your fingers are rusty with oxide.
Listen, can you hear the pigs,
Wessex Saddlebacks,
in their granite sty, snoring?

Can you shake your dusty wings
to fly with the rooster,
perch on the rotting haystack
warmed by early sun,
and summon up his voice
to clarion call the morning?

Meanwhile as you wake,
the farmer is mired in earth,
ironing the hills with his plough.
Open the windows, let curtains
flap. Call in fly-blown Friesians
to graze in bedrooms.
Will they search for new pasture,
or rest on green eiderdowns?

And now see the hawk-moth
as morning swims with mist
it shimmers into sight.
Turbo-charged, it seeks shelter
in valerian that sprouts white
and pink in the pig-sty wall.

When it dies, the rooster
offers it to his favourite bantam.

Ploughing stops at dusk.
The pigs are asleep again
their black eyelashes twitch
as they trot to the massage
parlour for a back scrub
and a kale smoothie.

Polly Stretton

Cœur Noir

1. Cœur Noir

Shabby pile of bones
under a black bridge.
You were found out;
talked to the hawk,
or a murder of crows.

Maybe his first love,
who found him
in flagrante
set him up,
or the second, the witness,
incredulous,
who did not wish
to believe.

Selfish, faithless,
he will be alone.
Codes and cryptography
won't help.
The black bridge
won't help,
it mocks,
celebrates bones,
droll bones,
beneath the bridge.

2. Cruel Bones

Soft feathers, cruel bones;
tender bones,
hard feathers under fallen acorns,
an arching oak, leaves golden.

Scrunched up heap
of debris, you will fade
by the time we know.
We'll talk to the hawk
or charming goldfinches.
Find out what's been done.
Spy until secrets are disclosed.

Little bird: bright red face,
long fine bill;
liquid song, positive, abundant,
your prosperous gold wing patch
will be missed
when it's time for milder climes.

But not you, pile of broken bones,
once flamboyant feathers, frail and friable
under a bridge.
You were a bird of infinite possibilities.
You've gone, though we can see
what you once were;
your colours fade
but we remember you.

3. The Hawk Returns

The hawk returns
all eyes and thighs.
Muscular legs, sharp talons,
beak curved for blood,
for tearing,
no sharing,
this one was his to destroy.

He caught you on the ground,
though it could have been sky,
his shadow overwhelmed.
His screams deafened you;
your stout heartbeat flickered in your breast,
the breast he tore with claws
that sliced through your song.

Small pile of bones,
bones and feathers under a bridge
beneath fallen acorns,
bruised as they fell,
scattered as they bounced
on hard feathers,
soft feathers, cruel bones;
tender bones, lurking beneath,
hiding under cover,
wings crossed over heart
protecting, defending, shielding
from the sharp-eyed hawk,

the powerful thighs that force,
the talons that tear you, wear you out
under golden leaves of arching oak.

4. Goldfinch are You Gone

Goldfinch, have you faded? Are you gone?
Or is there more to it than that?
Perhaps you lead us to discovery,
to find a truth,
to unearth, to learn, to recognise
that the hawk is as he is
despite appearing other.
His charm, his appeal, the magic
of his allure, his magnetism
will upbraid you, chastise you for believing
one so cold. He rebukes
your intrinsic belief in goodness,
chides you for childishness,
censures you for youth,
immaturity. It's how you've ended up
under the bridge.

Where I would praise you, goldfinch
for your faith, your trust,
your confidence, conviction
that there is good in all. Good in all.
Do you rely on that?
Did you rely on that?
You saw his eyes,

his thighs,
his disregard,
his coldness,
his wanton breach
and lack of devotion.
Yet loyalty led you to keep faith,
to be true, not to despair nor demand proof;
is this due to youth?

5. Unrestricted by Age

Oh, to be unrestricted by age,
to be able to see clearly,
not with doubting eyes but with eyes
unclouded by wishfulness,
free of blindfold fabric,
not dark but light and free,
open and at liberty
without being prevented
from understanding,
unblind, no longer visionless
sighted, open, unhampered
by the expectations
of the hawk.

6. Goldfinch Rising

There was a life for you,
little bird,
an other life for you.
You always knew, but sought excitement,
elated by the raptor's thrill of the chase.
Your little heart chuntered at the thought
he might leave if you did not surrender
to his superior id.

He wanted your prosperous slash of a gold wing patch,
your positivity, love of life,
he'd no knowledge of such things.
Your abundance showed him other ways.
He wanted to cling to your wings.
That didn't work.
His methods let him down;
allowed you to discover the predator that lurked,
ate at him, wanted your bones, your feathers,
the very essence of you.

So, you escaped.
You were a pile of bones under a bridge,
fallen on by acorns,
covered in golden leaves.
Now you rise.
Your broken wings mend,
your stout heartbeat returns,
shows the hawk there's more to belief

than cold, cruel cynicism pecking away at bones
under a bridge beneath an arching oak.
There is a life for you.
An other life for you.

Cate Cody

Brown and blue hues of estuaries

House Martins hang glide to feast,
whilst white waders fade into
one block, the
pristine flock dancing on notes
of quavered feet

the lip of mud is steep,
pummelled by the shouting tide;
its other side
smooth like a potter's beginning

we stand in the peace between
sky and water;
strands of hair
fight and flicker free
whilst we survey the estuary

Barbara Cumbers

Sutton Hoo

There is nothing here,
not now, and yet the nothing
of mounds, of grass, of stones,
is a presence still,

a king who faced two ways —
a cross and Woden's eye
both shining from a golden helmet;
Thor's hammer too,

three gods in one
in a ship interred in earth
and sailing nowhere. Wind beats
in waves across the grass,

light on the river in the valley
far from the nothing
of grass and stones that lies here
timeless, an unquiet voice.

Jenny Hamlett

She Drinks
Dartmoor

weaker now   we rest
beside the brook
in a sandy cutting

in this scarred place
the moor makes no promises

failure means a sheep's skull
a dead pony's stiff legs

at the top of the bank
a new foal waits

and here's his mother
coming at a fast trot ears pricked
alert   she see us   hesitates

but she must drink
there's been no rain

she slithers part way
down the steep slope   stops

slides down a little further
stops   we shrink
into stillness and silence

at last   fetlock deep in water
she drinks   pauses   lifts her head

shakes water beads from her muzzle
her bay coat shining with water light

she drinks again
and again as if
she had to empty Whitemoor Marsh

elderly
we plod slowly after them
as they trot away over the tinder-dry grass

but she whinnies as we pass
not panic   a greeting letting us know
we are welcome there

Geoff Chilton

Climbers at Yosemite

I
At El Capitan I see them staring,
eyes raised in calculation or prayer.
They mutter to themselves in low tones,
an arcane language I don't understand –
Gravity Ceiling, Gulf Stream, Tangerine Trip,
Prusik loop, arête.
They are granite-hard explanations of muscle
like rock ridges under tattoos and dreads.

II
He touches the stone. A beginning.
Perhaps feeling for weakness, a seduction?
Chalk-white fingers seeking holds and crevices,
suction of feet in black rubber shoes
that could have been made for dancing.
Then in a quick disturbance of muscles,
a lithe grasp of limbs
he magnetizes himself to the rock.

III
A clink of belay and carabiner
betrays him high up,
pressed against the face.
Squinting I spot him arachnid-stretched,
dayglo ropes looped and coiled,
chalk-bag dangling,
he ascends his own fear
while mist veils the mountain like death.

Sally James

Changing seasons

Stay with me my darling. I love your summer way.
I will try to re-capture you when autumn comes to stay.

Your warm caressing breezes have soothed me in my fear,
soft sunlight had lit up my life and dried the falling tear.

Oh, how you made the butterflies dance upon the flowers.
I've seen and heard the bees and birds while away their hours.

Their pollen laden wings, their fluttering and their song,
have eased and soothed the yearnings I've had so very long.

Now as cool rain is falling and ebbing in your wake
you are easing into autumn for your own sad shadow's sake.

When fall appears I know she'll be clothed in many a hue,
when she arrives in splendour, she'll be greeted just like you.

We are all just like the seasons, like them we ebb and flow
for we cannot stay forever, sometimes we must let go.

Yet memories will remain, they rest within our heart.
So, cherish them and nourish them so we may never part.

Nigel Kent

Cold water

A jolt

as fierce
as the electric punch
of a defibrillator.

It IS you

not one of your imposters
who snag the eye
in busy streets,
café windows,
supermarket queues.

We talk
tiptoeing
through the rubble
of our past

careful not to wake
recriminations
that roam its waste

and when provoked
bolt from shadows
snapping and snarling.

I dare to lead you

to where the future flows,
its currents strong and fast,
not suitable for those
who want to paddle
or tread water.

I leap in
inviting
you

to join me

but you decline.

It's far too deep,
too treacherous,
and anyway, you say,
you never liked swimming;
it is such a solitary pastime.

Ian Ledward

The Wriggling River

Or, it could have been 'The best poem I've never written about the River Earn.'

This quicksilver serpent,
this creation born in mist,
flows and eddies, and in its passage
spews the nooks and crannies
where letters gather in puddles.

Behind rocks and broken branches
they collect, whirling like wheels,
words forming like whorls on thumbs
in the curls and coils
of an obscure language,
then swallowed again in its ever moving,
ever searching, maelstrom of
omnivorous mouths,

Swirling from familiarity
into illegible spirals, then
unfurling and twisting again
into strings of comprehension,
just for a moment…

…then, stolen away in the diddles and duddles
of its current.

Things form.
Agonisingly near.

Phrases paraphrase themselves;
becoming solidly familiar
yet untouchably distant,
taunting in their intangibility,
caught in the tangle of a net
that dissolves itself into its spaces.

If only I could extend the fingers
of my mind and catch an end
and pull it in,
but it slips away
and is gone again in this wriggling river.

Julie Anne Gilligan

Reflection 2

There comes a time
to draw some lines
where you can no longer say
'I'll leave it 'til another day.'
There may not be another
Or you'll have a different
kind of bother
when feet won't work
or eyes play dumb.
So, say now 'I did that then
and it was good!
But I can't go there again.'

M. C. Gardner

All rules are suspended

once a year…in the lagoon…
a carnival of costumes –

the Moon in darkness
vaults over bridges
across dreams pulled taut
by an improvised wind
in gondolas of pleasure

Marilyn Francis

Summer seasonal affective disorder

there will come a day in June when
even yellow socks and red crocs
will fail to pull you out of
a sun-obscuring mind fog
will fail to eclipse
the dusty shroud
that buries
volition
paralyses
intent

and nothing
can be done
the grey blanket
has descended
and the books
from birthdays
and Christmases
long past
remain
unread
and days waste
playing patience
and looking out
of the window
and nothing is right

you are the fly in the butter
the wasp in the beer
the ants at a picnic
and nothing
seems to fit

Katherine Rawlings

TEATIME

The smell of baked bread would welcome me
as my grandmother bustled round her kitchen.
The bread generously sliced, still warm,
the crust crisp to the bite,
spread thick with churned butter from the nearby dairy
and the love in her sweet smile.
On bread baking day the tea was always
a grand, singularly sweet treat:
the marmalade made from lemons picked from a tree
carefully nurtured in her greenhouse,
or jams made from her own fruits,
especially plump strawberries, or raspberries from her kitchen
                                                                                              garden.
This was enjoyed with her inimitable blend
brewed in her big, brown teapot.
'Never forget that extra spoonful of leaves for the pot.' she said.
The milk jug was covered with a lace doily of her own design.
I have it still.
The smell of baking bread drifting in on the breeze
from the town bakery through my kitchen window,
seems always to whisper to me,

'Eat up, my love.'

Alice Harrison

Silver

Evelyn Homer Beckett,
teacher in the Welsh Grammar,
that thought itself a public school,
in her classically tailored Gor-Ray skirt,
academic gown slipping over her shoulder,
told the girl to go to the cloakroom
and put a comb through her hair.
The girl, already feeling gawky, inferior
and in awe of the teacher, burned with mortification
and didn't have a comb.

Another day after some misdemeanour,
instead of lines or detention
Miss Beckett gave the girl
a poem by Walter de la Mare to learn.
After a dutiful, word-perfect recitation,
expecting dismissal, the girl was surprised
to be questioned about her feelings for the poem
and for other poems to be recommended.
Instead of the anticipated humiliation
she felt, somehow, appreciated.

Ian Campbell

The End

The time will come as such times do
When fate will call a halt
My bass drum heart shall pump no more
The back beat like it ought
My eyes will stare at nothing then
My lungs will both deflate
My pulse will draw a whining line
I'll be described as 'late'.

The present and the future then
Will suddenly be past
Be snowballed to a rising hill
The first stage of the last
And all those memories I had
That only I recalled
Will dissipate like sunlit cloud
They won't be there at all.

And Talfourd, Amott, Friary Road
Would suddenly be zapped
All this to me, the history,
Just straight lines on a map
Soon all this stuff, including me,
Would snap and disappear
You'll wonder sometimes, lost in thought,
If we were ever here.

So, in the meantime I must try
To leave a lasting note
A legacy of tenancy
An anecdote to quote
For when the coffin lid is nailed
All that shall exist
Is photographs and memories
And poetry like this.

Title nicked from Wilfred Owen but it's all about my death, whenever that is.

K. J. Barrett

Wounded In Action

I had a tiny hole in my head,
My horse lying on top of me
Lashed out one last time before dying,
I couldn't control the cavalry boot
With the leg in it,
Which was moving too far away,
I tried to say something,
But my mouth was stiff with blood,
I wanted to ask how was it
That the sun and moon
Were both shining at the same time,
I wanted to point at the sky
But my arm wouldn't move,
The huge shadows
Were growing all around me,
And on the grass
Two Russian officers
Were dancing as in a ballet.
And what on earth was I to do
With the scent of flowers
Whose name I couldn't remember.

Wendy Goulstone

Jubilation 1945

The year in which I was seven years old and my mother
took me with her to the Odeon to watch the Pathe newsreel
and said 'don't look' too late, I saw the skeletal people,
their skin tight against their ribs, their eyes staring from skulls.

The year my mother and I waited to catch the bus to town,
her ration book secured in the inner pocket of her handbag,
and a woman opened her door and shouted 'The war is over!'
200,000 people, or more, died in Japan.

The year my mother took down the blackout curtains,
and voted Conservative, while my dad voted Labour,
putting Churchill out of business and Attlee in power,
a man and his wife committed suicide in Nazi Germany.

The year my sister and I walked round the streets after dark
and looked through people's windows to see the lights,
fifty nations signed the United Nations Treaty
and the Cold War began.

The year we had the street party, and all the mothers
wore their best aprons to serve us jam sandwiches and jelly,
Animal Farm was published, we wept over Brief Encounter,
and we thought there would be no more wars.

Jim Lindop

Gooseberry Pie

As we crossed the emptied fields
just now and four larks chattered
and a breeze sauntered
through the whitened stalks,
and the old church wallowed
in self-satisfaction,
I remembered another walk,
but one when I was maybe eight…
…or nine…and Tommy'd said
this was the gate…mossed, unlatched,
awry, grassed to our scabby knees,
an oval whitened notice half-attached,
and banks of cow-parsley shifting,
and posts that dogs had used.

And she came to us, dogs tacking
behind her paisley-printed dress
and sweat-stained oxters
and unattended long brown hair
and asked us in a voice that was a song
if we'd like some gooseberry pie.

Phil Craddock

Grace

After perching for some fifteen minutes
on a water container anchoring
a corner of the hospitality tent
on the leafy, shaded, quieter side
of The Long Walk, I found myself approached
by a woman wearing a full-length dress
with a breezy pattern of bold, bright colours
and a Union flag for a shawl.

But instead of gliding across the ground
as somehow would have seemed appropriate
she was stooped, plodding and hoping out loud
to find (just as I had) somewhere to sit.
I stood up and said, 'Please use this.'
'But that is yours.' 'I've rested enough.'
And as she thanked me, I complimented her
on her extraordinary gown.

'I took it up a little last night.' she said,
'I wore it to the lying-in-state last week.
I was number three in the queue, you know,
at Lambeth Bridge, with my Welsh friend Annie.
We were passing by and saw a lady
standing alone. Vanessa from Sri-Lanka.
And we decided to stay and keep her
company. We were there two whole nights.'

'It rained the second night. Just a drizzle
but they were kind enough to take us
to St Thomas' Hospital to dry off.
It was lovely to be able to pay our respects
to the Queen. She was always there for us.
So, of course I had to be here as well
to see the hearse pass by.' A pause.
'I'm sorry about my voice.'

Her voice had a glorious, happy lilt
but was syncopated with halts and coughs.
'It's all the interviews – questions, questions.
I'm from Mitcham, but originally Ghana.'
I asked her if she would like a coffee.
'So kind, yes please. A latte, three sugars.'
It took some time (there was quite a long queue)
and when I returned, she was holding court

with a squad of marshals clearly also
captivated by her attire. We resumed
our conversation, but as I was
finding it more and more difficult
to attune to her accent (music though it was)
and not wanting to keep on asking her
to repeat herself, being aware that
she could instead be resting her voice,

I took her hand, said, 'A pleasure to meet you.'
and backed off into the vast ranks of crowds
to see what the massive TV screens
were broadcasting now of the day's events.
As the coffin floated out of Westminster
Abbey and sailed serenely through
the suburbs of London, I suddenly felt
the loss of someone I never really knew.

Kate Young

Negative Space

Leafing through photos
my fingers trace
the shape of your smile
ghosting the Royal Mile.
Edinburgh: March 2007

Eyes scan a vibrant print,
coloured glass flooding
the Sagrada Familia, marble
smooth as your luminous skin.
Barcelona: March 2008

A yellow taxi, arm raised,
voices caught in New York roar
we tumble in, you in sepia
invisible on vacant leather.
5th Avenue: March 2009

Overexposed, light catches us
dazzled by the van Gogh,
sunflower gold in my hair
wispy gossamer air in yours.
The National Gallery: March 2010

A close-up snap on a beach.
We are laughing, rain dripping
from plastic, your waxy sheen fading
like the places you've never been.
Cromer: March 2011

The 6-year anniversary
all of us in our usual seats
the empty space to my right
inviting me to fill in the gaps.
Kent: March 2012

An image tumbles free,
my daughter's fingers
reaching for yours, inching
through the negative space.
The hospice: March 2006

Nigel Pearce

When Mother Died

The black clams of Time stuck onto Mum's frail body,
those rusty chains of age and illusion bound her mind.
She spiralled inwards in an introspective frenzy of sparks.
As her autumn leaves were blown into the chill of winter,
I walked with her and her ghosts in that becalmed Odyssey.
Slimy sea monsters would rise and frighten us, both children,
Mum and I would sit in the House of Dementia; she sat hunched
yet meditating on the coloured, interwoven threads of her
                                                  memories.
The wind blew her, that crumpled paper Buddha, away into
                                                  infinity.

Rob Lowe

EXTINGUISHED?

The fire extinguisher behind its glass
On the ninety-nine Darlington bus
Was like the image of a photograph,
Above a body sleeping under stone.
But should we break and resurrect its jet,
It falls in incandescence of the flame
It dances with to death, subsides in foam.

Unlike the name of a loved one that became
Not the flickering temporary ghost of a life,
But a script curled in a wick, waiting to be lit.

Hilary Mellon

IN DEATH

suddenly
    today I feel you
        sliding into my mind
            as easily and exquisitely
                as you did into my body

and now
    years of memories
        sound-tracked
           with your familiar voice
                unspool themselves inside my head

Julie Stamp

Looking for Hardware

At dad's request, I would plumb the depths
of his scratched metal tool box for a tack
exactly this long, a nail as wide as that
or a screw with a cross on its head, not a line.
'Mind your fingers', he would say,
'There are a lot of sharp things in there.'

It was the non-tools that appealed the most:
sheets of sandpaper worn sealskin-smooth,
a shrivelled chamois or a squat brass drawing pin.
Best of all was a twirl of plastic-coated wire,
cartoon-bright amongst all the pewter, copper, grey.

Sneaking a sideways glance at dad, I would heft
the heavy horseshoe magnet up from the depths,
hardware lodged like limpets to its girth,
then test the pull/repel of its poles
with a hair-slide, press stud or buckle.

Sometimes he would 'drop' a handful of tacks
onto the cracked lino floor, asking if I might
pick them up with the magnet,
'Seeing as I had it to hand.'

Such times were golden and gleam among the rusted,
the misshapen; times riven by deep cuts
like the cross on a Phillips-head screw.
The polar force of memory pulls back through,
draws out the treasure, lifts it from the dross.

Ali Chakir

How the world can decrease and expand

Walking ten miles a day
my mother went over the hills with the dog,
around the golf course perimeter
on over the river, in and out of the villages
heading back to town,
stopping to chat,
collecting stories from strangers
to bring home and share.
Later a five-yard box was her limit,
encompassing a commode, a chair and a cot,
blind and deaf in both ears,
slowly shrinking to fit her own coffin.
Lost in dementia her mind expanded,
dreaming of visits to Scotland
and driving in Wales,
walking through memories,
cycling forgotten lanes,
waiting at imaginary bus stops
for the bus that never showed up,
meeting old friends, angels and strangers.
Confined she was not.

Lindsay Rossdale

Villanelle: Passing Through

The only one you travel with is you
You may go faster, further, even higher
The same door opens on a different view

If all you want is something always new
How will you even know your heart's desire?
The only one you travel with is you

For every win a reckoning is due
So fully understand what you acquire
The same door opens on a different view

Remember that true friends are far and few
Be careful whom you welcome at your fire
The only one you travel with is you

You won't remember all that you've been through
But tell your stories knowing you're a liar
The same door opens on a different view

No longer sure that anything is true
Or if you are the merchant or the buyer
The only one you travel with is you
The same door opens on a different view

Poets

Name	Page	Name	Page
Denis Ahern	20	Susan Jarvis Bryant	22
Jane Avery	24	Nigel Kent	46
Pru Bankes Price	16	Ian Ledward	48
K. J. Barrett	58	Jim Lindop	60
Liz Beber	18	Rob Lowe	67
Ian Campbell	56	Karen Macfarlane	10
Ali Chakir	70	Ross McGivern	29
Geoff Chilton	44	Hilary Mellon	68
Cate Cody	40	Peter Meredith-Smith	14
Phil Craddock	61	Suzie Millar	21
Barbara Cumbers	41	Vicki Morley	31
Tim Field	19	Kewal Paigankar	26
Marilyn Francis	52	Madeline Parsons	11
Christine Frederick	8	Nigel Pearce	66
M. C. Gardner	51	Katherine Rawlings	54
Julie Anne Gilligan	50	Lindsay Rossdale	71
Wendy Goulstone	59	Sue Spiers	25
Adrian Green	12	Julie Stamp	69
Jenny Hamlett	42	John Starbuck	7
Alice Harrison	55	Polly Stretton	33
John Hughes	28	Kate Young	64

Acknowledgements:

Summer seasonal affective disorder by Marilyn Francis was published in Vole Books, *Washed With Noon - poems from the VOLE Summer Competition 2023*, selected by Richard Hawtree, edited by Janice Dempsey.

Jazz at The Royal – Now and Then by Adrian Green was broadcast on BBC Essex, 1 June 2023 and is included in *New Blues and Other Poems* (Littoral Press 2023).

Cold Water by Nigel Kent is included in *Fall,* Nigel Kent, Hedgehog Poetry Press, 2023.

The Wriggling River by Ian Ledward was published in *Dreich* 2 Season 8 (No. 86) - in March 2024.

Coeur Noir by Polly Stretton, Section 1 was first published in *The Alchemy of 42* by Black Pear Press 2020.

Milton Keynes UK
Ingram Content Group UK Ltd.
UKHW021847060724
445042UK00015BA/857